CHARLES C. MANZ

The POWER of FAILURE

27 Ways to
Turn Life's Setbacks into
Success

BK

BERRETT-KOEHLER PUBLISHERS, INC.
San Francisco

Berrett-Koehler Publishers, Inc.
235 Montgomery Street, Suite 650
San Francisco, CA 94104-2916
Tel: 415-288-0260   Fax: 415-362-2512
Website: www.bkconnection.com

First edition publised by Berrett-Koehler Publishers, Inc., San Francisco
All rights reserved.
©2001 by Charles M. Manz

This Edition not for distribution in or to bookstores.

Printed By: Triumphant Publishers International
          P.O.Box 2650
          Broken Arrow, OK 74012

Printed in the United States of America

 Printed on acid-free and recycled paper that is composed of 85 percent recovered fiber, including 10 percent postconsumer waste.

Library of Congress Cataloging-in-Publication Data
Manz, Charles C.
   The power of failure : 27 ways to turn life's setbacks into success / by Charles C. Manz.
        p.   cm.
   Includes bibliographical references and index.
   ISBN 1-57675-132-5
   1. Success.   2. Failure (Psychology).   I. Title.
   BJ1611.2.M337 2001
   158.1—dc21   2001043753

06 05 04 03 02   10 9 8 7 6 5 4 3 2 1

Copyeditor: Patricia Brewer
Text design: Detta Penna
Compositor/production service: Penna Design & Production
Indexer: Joan Dickey

I dedicate this book
to those truly successful people
who have made the world a better place
by standing a little taller each time
they picked themselves up after falling
and who gained the wisdom
and humility from these experiences
to help others
to do the same.

Contents

Part Three
Coping with Failure   73

Part Four
Collaborating with Failure   105

Getting Started:
The Power of Failure Motto   133

Preface

At the outset a question comes to mind, "Why write a book focused on failing?" First, as you will soon discover, this book is actually a book on a primary secret to success—how to harness the **Power of Failure**. Nevertheless, the real motivation that led me to write this book is more personal. On many occasions people have said to me something like, "You are obviously a very successful person. Don't you ever fail at anything?" By outward appearances, my life may seem to be mostly filled with success, such as having published 12 books and 100 articles or having received a number of awards during my academic career. But frankly I find this kind of comment rather embarrassing.

I'm embarrassed because I know what they

apparently don't: that I have failed far more than I have succeeded. Sometimes people point to one of my previous books. They may point to the success of *SuperLeadership: Leading Others to Lead Themselves* that I co-authored with my good colleague Hank Sims, Jr., which won a national book award and became a national best-seller. They just see the end result, but I remember how many times we rewrote chapters that weren't working and the fact that the book was rejected by about 30 publishers before finally being signed by a risk-taking young editor. The truth is that the book almost never saw the light of day.

Or they might point to my career as a professor. I am very fortunate and honored to currently hold the Nirenberg Chair of Business Leadership at the University of Massachusetts. And I previously held appointments at several major universities, including a Marvin Bower Fellowship at the Harvard Business School that was awarded for, in their words, "outstanding achievement in research and exceptional promise . . . in business scholarship." What people don't know is that I struggled a great deal in my early career, first to find a job at all after college and then both in retailing (I truly failed relative to most standards in that brief experience) and in my early years as a young professor. It would be difficult for me to even calculate how many papers I have had rejected by journals, how many students didn't care for my teaching style, and how many business executives found my consulting to be less than exceptional.

Don't get me wrong; I'm not saying that I consider myself a failure in work and life. On the contrary, I consider myself to be a considerable success. When people say that they think I am a successful person, that is not what I find embarrassing. It's that they seem to think I do not, never have, and apparently never will, fail in significant ways. What I am saying is that I truly believe that I owe most of the success I have enjoyed to my willingness to fail, to fail repeatedly, and to fail well. That is really why I am writing this book: to give failure the credit it deserves and to hopefully help others discover the rich rewards it offers when it is handled wisely.

This short book is filled with simple ideas about how to use failure in the short run in order to succeed on a long-term basis, throughout a lifetime. It is written for anyone who would like to increase his or her awareness and ability to reap the rewards of the many inevitable failures that we all experience in our lives. This recognition can be a very freeing experience. It can feel wonderful to drop the heavy weight of trying to explain away our human fallibility, of feigning perfection, and of denying that when we take risks and try new worthwhile things we will surely make mistakes.

Of course, some mistakes should not be made,

such as when we recklessly endanger the lives of others. At the same time, when we sincerely do our best with good intentions and come up short, it rarely does much good to dwell on our immediate failure. If we really want to do better next time around, it is far better to reframe our view. It is not that we have failed and that is the end of the story but that we are in the ongoing developmental process of succeeding. I hope that by the time you finish this book you will enjoy many of the benefits that flow from learning this ultimate secret—the way to realize meaningful success is to harness the **Power of Failure**.

Acknowledgments

I would like to thank the friends and colleagues who have significantly affected my thinking about life and work in ways that helped me to arrive at *The Power of Failure* philosophy, especially the role that learning and development play in moving from setbacks to success. They include Hank Sims Jr., Chris Neck, Greg Stewart, Vikas Anand, Bob Marx, Jim Mancuso, Bob Mitchell, Peter Hom, Frank Shipper, Tedd Levitt, Tom Thompson, Tedd Mitchell, Chris Argyris, Richard Hackman, Denny Gioia, Ed Lawler, Kathi Lovelace, John Newstrom, Mike Beyerlein, Fred Luthans, Bill Glick, John Sheridan, Art Bedeian, Kevin Mossholder, Andy Van de Ven, Hal Angle, Mary Nichols, John Slocum, Mike Mahoney, and my wife and co-author, Karen Manz.

In addition, I thank the University of Massachusetts at Amherst, and especially my Dean and Department Chairs in the Isenberg School of Management, Tom O'Brien, Bill Wooldridge, and Linda Smircich. The Administrative Resources Center, and especially Becky Jerome, have been very helpful with preparing my book manuscripts over the past few years. Special thanks go to Charles and Janet Nirenberg, whose generous gift made possible my current position as the Nirenberg Professor of Business Leadership.

I am also very grateful for the encouragement, support, and assistance I received from my editor Steven Piersanti and the very competent, wise, and compassionate staff at my publisher, Berrett-Koehler. Finally, I express my appreciation to all my other friends, colleagues, and to my extended family who have provided encouragement and support for me and my work through my many failures and successes over the years.

Charles C. Manz
February 2002

Introduction

Succeeding with the Power of Failure

Only he who does nothing makes no mistakes.
—French Proverb[1]

Would you like to be successful throughout the remainder of your life? Would you like to enjoy meaningful success where you learn, grow, and contribute in significant ways; where your life is full, counts for something, and makes a difference? If your answer is "yes," then you must fail. There is no exception to this rule. *Significant success requires failure*, but failure must be regarded in a whole new light. That is what this book is about—how to use the *Power of Failure* to Succeed.

Failure is one of the most dreaded words in the English language. The very idea of failing is enough to stop most people in their tracks. It can cause the majority to simply pack up, turn around, and retreat without even trying.

Success, on the other hand, is nearly a magical idea for most people. The possibility of succeeding or becoming a "success" is an almost mythical pursuit. People love to be labeled a success and will often sacrifice greatly to achieve this end.

Although most people hate to be labeled a failure and love to be labeled a success, it is only through seeming failure that most of life's greatest successes are achieved. Usually, "failure" or "success" is almost entirely in the eye of the beholder.

As an example, who can forget the classic children's story *The Ugly Duckling* by Hans Christian Andersen? One of the birds in a community of ducks is singled out for constant ridicule because he is so different from the rest. He is treated as an utter failure and comes to view himself as exactly that. Consequently, he loses his sense of hope, falls into despair, and runs away from his troubles.

Eventually the Ugly Duckling learns that his difference is not the curse that he thought it was. In fact, when he finally sees his own reflection in a pond and discovers that he is a magnificent swan, his apparent failure in life is completely transformed.

This story may reflect an essential truth about what we call "failure." It is very often a misperception about the difference between what exists and goes unnoticed (such as growth and learning when we fall short of reaching a goal) and what is realized later (longer term success).

Of course, sometimes failure is tied to a lack of competence to perform in the face of a specific challenge, but seeming failures can be a powerful way to learn and ironically provide the means for life's greatest breakthroughs and successes. Eventually we can learn to accept that what most people call failures are usually only temporary setbacks in relation to some arbitrary standard and are an essential part of life. They are usually just *challenges in progress*. This important lesson can help us understand that the only real failures occur when we back away from worthwhile challenges without even trying or when we refuse to learn from our setbacks.

Changing our perspective is often the key to finding success in seeming failure. Optimistic thinking has sometimes gotten a bad rap as being unrealistic, but research has found that we can indeed live happier, healthier, and more successful lives if we can learn to discover the opportunities in problems. These problems then become merely challenging opportunities that we can turn to our advantage. They provide opportunities for personal growth and can stimulate our creativity for finding better ways to live.

In the end, the Ugly Duckling makes this kind of discovery and is magnificently transformed. Then he is able to take flight as the beautiful swan that he is and soar high above the ducks that had treated him with such disdain. We too can more fully live as the magnificent beings that we are if we can come to see that:

- Challenges are disguised opportunities

- Differences are a gift

- Mistakes are learning opportunities

- When we try our best and are willing to learn, we always succeed, even if we don't achieve the results we hoped for.

This book is designed to provide simple yet profound ways to turn seeming failures into successes. It contains practical prescriptions for successfully meeting some of life's most common setbacks. The lessons of this book are organized into four parts. They include redefining success and failure, winning through losing, coping with failure, and collaborating with failure. It will become obvious that these four parts, while distinct, are also highly related and that the lessons contained in each significantly overlap. Nevertheless, it is useful to consider the various prescriptions that this book has to offer across these four key areas for turning failure into success.

It is also helpful to think of the various specific lessons of this book in relation to a larger whole—more general guidelines for failing successfully. Most of the book's prescriptions relate to some primary themes, which are summarized in the following list. We can think of these themes as a new view or vision of how we can transform failure so that it contributes positively to more successful living.

A New View of Failure: Some Primary Themes

1. **Redefine Failure.** Failure is a natural part of life that can impact us positively or negatively depending on how we define it.

2. **Redefine Success.** The more important measure of success is based on our own deeper knowing of what's right for us rather than approval or disapproval from others.

3. **Learn from Failure.** Failure presents an opportunity for continued learning and growth while success can lead to complacency and stagnation.

4. **View Failures as Stepping-Stones to Success.** Success and failure are not incompatible—most failures are simply *challenges in progress* that can provide a foundation for success.

5. **Find the Opportunities of Failure.** Setbacks or short-term failures can contribute to future success if we focus on the opportunities they contain rather than the obstacles.

6. **Use Negative Feedback to Your Advantage.** Current negative feedback can provide positive

information for improvement or may even suggest that you are onto something new and different—a sign of a pending breakthrough success.

7. **Look Beyond Yourself.** As you learn to focus outward, on helping others succeed rather than yourself, you become less vulnerable to what otherwise might appear to be personal failures.

8. **Persist.** Keep on trying and trying. *Sustained Effort + the Lessons of Failures* is a powerful formula for success.

One other point should be made at the outset. This book is not advocating failure as end in itself. Rather, failure is a means, an essential ingredient, to successful living. The value of failure is in the learning and growth that it provides. Without learning and growth, failure can be a destructive force in our lives. In that sense this book is really about effective success, not success that leads to an inflated self-image and complacency, but rather success as a way of living that benefits from all life has to offer. And that includes successful learning in the face of setbacks and what some mislabel as failure.

The lessons of this book can help us find the opportunities that are just waiting to be discovered in the challenges and "failures" we face every day. They offer *prescriptions for a more productive, prosperous, and peaceful life.* This book is about failure, but failure seen in a whole new light. It is about how we can harness the *Power of Failure* to help us succeed.

To help get this process started, old and new definitions of failure and success follow. I hope that by the end of this book the new definitions of success and failure will become a natural part of your perspective of life.

Failure

Old Definition

A negative, fatal, and final result indicating:

- An inability to perform and a lack of success

- A falling short because of ineptness, deficiency, or negligence

- A bad, bad thing that should be avoided, mourned, and punished.

New Definition

A short-term unexpected result that reflects a challenge in progress and that provides:

- A stepping-stone to success

- An opportunity for learning and development

- An opportunity for creative change and innovation.

Success

Old Definition

A revered shrine of achievement.
An all-positive final result indicating:

- Superior ability that requires no further learning or change

- Performance that is devoid of flaws, weakness, or failure

- A good, good thing that should be sought, celebrated, and honored above all else.

New Definition

A way of living founded on benefiting from all life has to offer that is:

- A long-term sequence of life-improving results

- An outcome of short-term setbacks and failures

- A process of continual development, learning, and fulfillment in life.

If you can dream —
and not make dreams your master;

If you can think —
and not make thought your aim;

*If you can **meet with***
Triumph and Disaster

And treat those two impostors
just the same . . .

—From "If" by Rudyard Kipling

Part
One

Redefining Failure and Success

Failure is not something to be feared. It contains a positive challenge for successful living. Today's failures contain the seeds of tomorrow's greatest successes. The first step to mastering the art of failing successfully is to come to see failure and success in a whole new light.

To Succeed More, Fail More

*Failure is the foundation of success,
and the means by which it is achieved.*
—*Lao Tzu*[2]

An aspiring young man once asked a very prominent CEO how he could become more successful. The CEO was Tom Watson of IBM, who reportedly responded that if the young man wanted to become more successful he should do the seemingly unthinkable—fail. In fact, Watson advised that he should *double his failure rate*. At first glance this is an odd prescription indeed. Upon closer inspection, however, it contains a great deal of wisdom.

A failure should not be viewed as the end of the story but instead as a stepping-stone to a larger success. If someone never fails, this is a telltale sign that he is not trying anything new or challenging. Mastering new skills and growing as individuals require that we enter unfamiliar arenas that can provide us with new knowledge and capabilities. These new ventures can be as varied as learning to play the piano, speak a foreign language, water-ski, or invest in the stock market.

The principle remains the same—you must experience failure in order to succeed. If you expect to learn without making a mistake, you are in for an unpleasant surprise. Imagine Mozart or Beethoven trying to compose music so cautiously that they never hit a wrong note. Do you think they would have been able to compose masterpieces if they totally avoided mistakes?

In fact, Beethoven was no stranger to failure. At one stage in his music career a music teacher said that he had no talent for music. The teacher even remarked that "as a composer he is hopeless."

The more you try to grow your knowledge and experience in new and challenging areas, the more mistakes you will have to make. Much of this potential for growth boils down to being willing to take risks. Author Carole Hyatt wrote that aggressive CEOs will tell their direct reports: "If you haven't failed at least three times today you haven't tried anything new." And she adds that avoiding failure leads to avoiding risks—"a type of behavior not well suited to most businesses in today's economy."[3] So if you want to succeed more quickly, heed the surprisingly sage advice—*double your failure rate.*

If you want to be more successful ...
"double your failure rate."

Be a Successful Learner by Learning from Failure

B ill Gates provided a practical perspective on the importance of learning from failure in his book *Bill Gates @ the Speed of Thought*, "Once you embrace unpleasant news not as negative but as evidence of a need for change, you aren't defeated by it. You're *learning* from it."[4,5] He then went on to list many costly Microsoft product failures that provided the learning and opportunity for development of many of Microsoft's biggest successes, mentioning the following examples:

- Many apparently wasted years working on a failed database called Omega resulted in the development of the most popular desktop database, Microsoft Access.

- Millions of dollars and countless hours invested in a joint operating system project with IBM that was discontinued led to the operating system Windows NT.

- A failed multiplan spreadsheet that made little headway against Lotus 1-2-3 provided learning that helped in the development of Microsoft Excel, an advanced graphic spreadsheet that leads the competition.

Clearly Bill Gates had a view of successful learning from setbacks that helped him and his company to turn many potential failures into dynamic successes.

Without a doubt one of the most powerful pillars of long-term success is learning from mistakes. The importance of learning from mistakes for achieving significant success is so widely recognized that it might almost seem unnecessary to mention. A challenging, well-lived, and successful life will be filled with both ups and downs. Growing as a person and addressing significant real-world problems means we will surely fail some of the time, but if we learn from these failures and stay the course, we will eventually succeed.

Effective learning of challenging activities largely depends on how we think about failure. Just as we develop habits in our behavior, we also develop habits in our thoughts. And many of us have powerful thought habits about failure that include negativity and self-criticism and these demoralize us. The result is that we impede the very learning that we need to help things work out better the next time around. The challenge is to manage our thoughts about failures in such a way that we learn from them and consequently increase our personal effectiveness in our work and life.

If we can concentrate on learning from every situation, especially those in which we seem to fail, we will continually move ahead. This effective approach might be called learning forward. How can we learn forward through failures? To begin with, view short-term failures as the building blocks for future success and concentrate on learning all you can from them rather than trying to make excuses or trying to cover up these temporary setbacks. The trick is to always move forward as you fail.

For example, golfers would choose progressively more difficult courses and try more challenging shots as they progress in their game. At first, a relatively easy course and making conservative shot selections may represent the right amount of challenge. Over time, more difficult courses and more aggressive shots (trying to shoot over the trees rather than playing it safe and going around them) can be chosen. Undoubtedly the greater challenge will bring with it more mistakes and setbacks, but learning will increase as well.

As you master this process you can purposely choose new and greater challenges to learn from throughout your life that stretch you more and more. Fail at greater and greater worthwhile challenges, and you can learn on your way to ultimate long-term success.

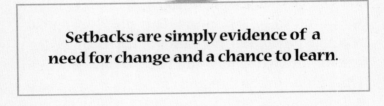

Setbacks are simply evidence of a need for change and a chance to learn.

3

Recognize Failure as the Lifeblood of Success

We can take a variety of roads in the pursuit of success. One obvious route is to work toward a goal as unerringly as possible until it is achieved. Success is measured by our clear progress toward this end. Failure is not only left out of the equation but it is avoided above all else. It is seen as incompatible with success.

Unfortunately, this all too dominant perspective can create some real problems in terms of our ability to learn, to grow, and to take the necessary risks we need to be fully alive. In his book *The Active Life,* noted author Parker Palmer powerfully addresses this concern. He points out that in the West our fixation on success (or what he refers to as "instrumental action"):

discourages us from risk-taking because it values success over learning, and it abhors failure whether we learn from it or not . . . [it] always wants to win, but win or lose, it inhibits our learning. If we win, we think we know it all and have nothing more to learn. If we lose, we feel so defeated that learning is a hollow consolation.

And as if this telling passage weren't enough he goes on to say:

[it] traps us in a system of praise or blame, credit or shame, a system that gives primacy to goals and external evaluations, devalues the gift of self-knowledge, and diminishes our capacity to take the risks that may yield growth.[6]

We can choose another road (perhaps Robert Frost's mythical road less traveled by) that brings us face to face with failure as a primary vehicle for success. On this road failure is viewed as the very lifeblood of success. Palmer's words point to this kind of view.

Soichiro Honda, the founder of Honda Motor Company, dramatically paints a vision of this alternative route to success. After growing up in an impoverished family in which several of his siblings died of starvation, Honda encountered dramatic setbacks—including the bombing of his original piston plant in 1945 and later its complete destruction by an earthquake. His personal philosophy of success despite, or perhaps because of, his difficult past embraces failure. When receiving an honorary doctorate at the University of Michigan he said in his speech: "Many people dream of success. To me success can only be achieved through repeated failure and introspection. In fact, success represents the one percent of your work that results from the ninety-nine percent that is called failure."[7]

Once again we come face to face with the challenging prospect that setbacks are an unavoidable part of everyday life. We all fail. And not just a little but a lot, especially if we are taking the risks and pursuing the learning of new skills that enable us to meet exciting and worthwhile challenges. We are called to accept the infusion that these challenging times can offer to the health of our journey toward success. The worthwhile journey toward a rich, meaningful, and rewarding life requires a willingness to receive a good dose of failure—the ironic lifeblood of success.

**Success is the 1% that results
from the 99% we call failure.**

Learn the Challenging Secret to Successful Failure...Patience

There is a powerful but challenging secret about the relationship of short-term failures to longer term successes. This secret is very difficult for many to accept and incorporate into their work and life, but it is an essential part of learning how to use the *Power of Failure*. The secret is *patience*.

In a recent interview for *Fast Company* magazine, Steve Ballmer, CEO of Microsoft, emphasized the importance of patience for succeeding in business.[8] He explained that products and businesses go through three phases: vision, patience, and execution. And he said the patience stage is the toughest and most uncomfortable.

The vision stage generates a great deal of excitement

and energy and the future looks promising. Eventually the final execution stage is a time of fine-tuning and figuring out how to be even more successful. Both the vision and execution stages can be very satisfying and comfortable. It's the middle "patience" stage that can be very difficult. Ballmer explains, "You have to cut out parts . . . react to what the market is telling you. You get into trouble if you assume that you're going to reach critical mass too quickly—because it's most likely that you won't. Through all these trials you can't lose patience."[9]

Ballmer notes that Microsoft's Windows software was no exception to this pattern. "Windows 1.0 wasn't a success. Windows 2.0 wasn't a success. It wasn't until we put out Windows 3.1 that we really had a big winner."[10]

He goes on to explain that the recent setbacks in the Internet economy reflect a transition from the vision stage to the patience stage. He also points out that many entrepreneurs cannot handle the patience stage. Many seemed to believe the vision stage would never end or that execution would immediately follow without a need for patience. He cited small Internet companies doing Superbowl ads as an example of this misguided viewpoint. In the end he suggests that employees and investors alike need to either be patient or get out of the business.

I suspect it is fairly easy for most to identify with the sage advice of Ballmer. Anytime we set out to learn or accomplish something new and significant we likely face the same three stages and especially the challenge of the need for patience. Personally, patience is a tough challenge for me as I find myself failing on my way to what I hope will be ultimate success in a variety of activities.

One of my recent efforts has been to learn Tai Chi. I had a vision of the strength, flexibility, calmness, and other health benefits I would soon be deriving and how I would master the technique through the help of a professional instructor and the use of videotapes. I really wanted to go from vision to execution and had little desire to endure the patience stage. Consequently, despite my instructor's advice that I take it slow and start by learning just one or two poses of the dozens that make up a single form (a series of moves that completes one exercise sequence), I proceeded to try to learn a whole form, which should normally take up to a year or more, in about a month.

In retrospect I have to laugh a little at myself for trying to learn too quickly and lacking the patience to learn at an effective pace. My teacher pointed out it would take a great deal of work to relearn the poses in a technically correct way.

He ended by citing an ancient wisdom story, whose essence went something like this. A martial arts student was studying a new set of movements under a master and asked how long it would take to learn the new skills. The master responded that it would take perhaps two years. Being a bit discouraged and impatient with this answer, the student asked how long it would take if he would study and work very very hard. To this the master responded that then it would take him about four years.

The implication is clear—if we want to ultimately succeed in a significant way, we need to accept and be patient with the learning and development that go along with facing challenges. The bridge between short-term failures and ultimate success is a challenging one, but it may well be the essential secret to success—it is *patience*.

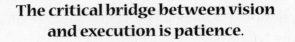

The critical bridge between vision and execution is patience.

5

Overcome the Success
Catch-22

In the classic American novel *Catch-22*, a pilot in World War II decides he does not want to continue flying combat missions.[11] He realizes the probability of being killed in action is high and feels that he has flown enough missions.

When he talks to the military doctor and requests to be grounded, the doctor explains that he cannot ground him based on his physical health. The pilot then claims to be "crazy" and requests to be grounded for psychological reasons. Despite the pilot's attempts to persuade him that he is crazy the doctor does not buy it. He also refuses to take the word of other bomber crew members who agree that the pilot is crazy. The doctor explains the crew members are the ones who are crazy because they don't ask to be grounded.

Ultimately, the doctor explains what he calls Catch-22: The pilot is *not* crazy because he asks to be grounded (a rational self-preserving wish) while the other crew members *are* crazy because they don't ask to be grounded (an irrational life-threatening choice). And the doctor does not ground those who don't ask to be grounded.

This comical paradox parallels one of the most difficult hurdles for people who want to be successful—what might be called the Success Catch-22. People who really want to be successful will be naturally resistant to failure. And yet we must fail, and usually many times, at least in the short run, if we are going to enjoy significant success in the long run.

For example, new employees hired into desirable jobs will likely want to be as successful as possible. They may go out of their way to avoid taking risks or doing anything that could jeopardize their new highly valued position. Wanting to be very successful can translate into a tendency to play it safe and not suffer any kind of failure.

The Success Catch-22 is that the more they want to succeed, the more they want to avoid the very kind of experiences (including well-fought failures) that will bring them the learning they need to be a long-term success. And good leaders will not let them escape these necessary developmental experiences (will not ground them) when they try to avoid challenging assignments or tasks that make setbacks more likely.

Taking on new challenges, stretching ourselves and growing as people, and learning significant new skills, can only be achieved with a good dose of failure along the way. Not failure that is final or sought for its own sake but failure that is a natural part of trying and learning new and challenging activities. We may want to be grounded from experiencing failure, but if we get our wish we will also be grounded from real success.

So what's the way out? It is to continually succeed even, perhaps especially, when we fail. We can succeed at learning, at persevering, and at continually growing and developing ourselves in the midst of what appears to be failure. So overcome the Success Catch-22 by learning to fail successfully over and over on the way to long-term success.

We tend to most resist failure when we most want to succeed . . . yet to succeed in new, challenging, and meaningful ways we must fail.

In the Face of Failure, Search for Opportunities, Not Obstacles

Ed Land, the inventor of instant photography and founder of Polaroid, kept a plaque on his wall that read "A mistake is an event, the full benefit of which has not yet been turned to your advantage."[12, 13] This kind of thinking is at the heart of harnessing the *Power of Failure*.

Indeed, our potential for success in life depends a great deal on the way we think. Focusing primarily on opportunities rather than obstacles, particularly in the failures we experience, is especially important. We can program ourselves to be "opportunity thinkers," but reprogramming our thinking is no easy task. Simply trying to think differently through force of will is generally not very productive. On the other hand, there are some practical things we can learn and do to help ourselves.

Dr. Albert Ellis, an authority on mental self-improvement therapy, maintains that beliefs can serve as a basis for change.[14] According to the underlying theory, when a person has difficulty coping with certain situations, this ineffectiveness can often be traced to irrational beliefs. For example, we might avoid trying a new activity such as skiing or tennis because we believe we will fail and embarrass ourselves. This is a form of obstacle thinking. Obstacle thinking is typically driven by fear, especially fear of failure. Only by challenging these dysfunctional beliefs, so the reasoning goes, can a person successfully deal with the problem.

If we realistically imagine and think through the challenge of skiing for the first time, and honestly face our doubts and fears, we have made a good start. Then by focusing on the opportunities for mastering a new skill and having an exhilarating experience we improve our chances of being successful. By purposely choosing thoughts, including imagining our eventual success and providing ourselves with inner encouraging self-talk ("this will be challenging but if I really concentrate and try my best I can do this . . ."), we create a mental foundation that can begin to replace our fears and doubts. Add to this the additional effort and practice that can flow from an optimistic expectation of our eventual success and we are well on our way to becoming a competent skier.

Substantial research has found that the way we think influences our health, longevity, performance, and many other aspects of successful living. Some of this research is a refinement of earlier work on self-fulfilling prophecies. According to Edward E. Jones, a psychologist at Princeton University, "Our expectancies not only affect how we see reality but also affect the reality itself."[15]

Dr. Martin Seligman, a leading researcher in this area, agrees: "My hunch is that for a given level of intelligence, your actual achievement is a function not just of talent, but also of the capacity to withstand defeat."[16] For example, in one study, Seligman found the way that insurance agents dealt with failures was often directly related to whether they became outstanding salespersons or quit the company. Those with an optimistic outlook sold 37 percent more insurance in their first two years than agents with pessimistic views. And the pessimists were twice as likely to quit in their first year. The key seems to be whether an individual will keep going when things get difficult, frustrating, and when effort results in failure.

Elbert Hubbard said, "The greatest mistake you can make in life is to be continually fearing you will make one."[17] A useful corollary to this might be "If you want to be successful in life, continually fill your mind with opportunities, not obstacles, so that you will create them."

Long-term success is largely influenced by our capacity to withstand defeat … and to focus on opportunities rather than obstacles.

To Be a Real Success, You Must Fail

The Introduction pointed out that most failures are simply challenges in progress. Whether these challenges ever arrive at success often depends on the strength and experience we bring to the challenge from struggling with past setbacks and failures.

Recently, a colleague e-mailed a revealing story that was circulating on the Internet about a butterfly. In the story, a man is watching a butterfly struggle to break out of its cocoon. After making some progress to work its way through a small hole, the butterfly appeared to simply stop its efforts. For some time it seemed to make no headway, so the man concluded it was stuck and decided to lend a helping hand by forming a larger opening in the cocoon with scissors.

Afterward the butterfly emerged easily but with small, shriveled wings and a swollen body.

It turned out that the struggle to emerge from the cocoon would have forced the fluid from the butterfly's body into its wings, a necessary process for enabling it to fly. As a result of the man's well-intentioned "help" he had interfered with nature's life-strengthening process. The butterfly was now doomed never to fly, but to crawl around with its swollen body and shriveled wings for the rest of its life.

Many of our failures in life present us with the same kind of challenge that the butterfly faced. Learning, personal growth, skill development, courage, persistence, the potential for empathy, and a host of other desirable life assets can be gained from failing successfully. We cannot hope to become really successful in our lives unless we learn to fail well in a way that prepares us for greater success. If we get caught in the trap of trying to avoid challenge and backing away from our setbacks, we cannot learn the valuable lessons that we need to learn. If we habitually explain away our short-term failures by making excuses and covering our tracks so that we always look successful, we stunt our personal growth. We need failures in life to provide us with the opportunity to wrestle with the kind of challenge that can squeeze the life-giving fluid we need to strengthen our wings for successful flight in life.

This is apparently the reason that NASA has used significant failure as an important criterion for selecting new recruits. When they were looking for potential astronauts for the Apollo 11 lunar mission, they invited resumes from the American public. They first weeded out applicants based on academic qualifications but they still had several thousand candidates.

The next step was a very interesting one. They weeded out all candidates who had not bounced back from a significant failure at some point in their careers. One might think it would be more logical to select those whose career performance was so strong that they had never experienced significant failure. They instead actually sought those who had failed. The apparent premise was that a person who had failed and then got up again was a stronger contender then one who had never experienced failure.[18]

Perhaps the best way to view this seemingly radical thinking at NASA would be to conclude that they wanted astronauts who had developed sufficient strength to withstand the many challenges of flying to the moon. Just like a butterfly that fully encounters the challenge of emerging from the cocoon, the ones who had struggled and recovered from failure were the ones viewed as having wings strong enough to take flight into space.

By wrestling with failure we grow strong wings for soaring to success.

Victory goes to the player who makes
the next-to-last mistake.

—*Savielly Grigorievitch Tartakower*[19]

**Part
Two**

Winning
through Losing

Sometimes the only sure way to win
in the long run is to lose in the short run.
Always striving to be the victor, being
right, receiving the award and recognition, can hold us back. Real winners learn
the art of winning through losing.

8

Sometimes When You Win, You Lose

Jon Bowen was running a 10K (6.2 miles) race, the Harvest Moon Classic, in Washington, D.C.[20] He had trained very hard for the race and was on target for a personal best time as he neared the halfway point. Suddenly, the runner in front of him twisted his ankle in a pothole and fell to the cement. The fallen runner grasped his ankle as he rolled onto his back. In one instant Mr. Bowen was faced with the decision whether to stop and help or run on past. He later explained that he had faced a moral dichotomy: "Duty to fellow man or every man for himself?"

He didn't stop. In fact, he hurdled the runner in an effort to avoid losing precious time. When he glanced over his shoulder he saw that a woman runner had stopped to lend a hand. In the end, Bowen did finish with his personal record, but it bothered him that he made, in his words, "the selfish choice."

Quoting novelist Ian McEwan, who wrote, "Selfishness is written in our hearts," Bowen said that he believes compassion is in our hearts too. The challenge when you are heading for the finish line, he explained, "is knowing when to let compassion take the lead. Next time I hope to make the right choice."[21]

A story like this invites us to rethink our definition of winning. To borrow a line from a popular movie, "sometimes when you win you lose. . . ."[22] Jon Bowen won in the sense that he ran the race in a personal best time but later recognized that he had lost in a deeper sense. He made a choice of short-sighted winning over a more lasting kind of victory.

Each of us encounters this kind of choice everyday. It can be an opportunity to lend a hand when someone needs our help at work or to stop what we are doing and listen when a friend needs someone to talk to. Making the right choice when it temporarily distracts from our progress is the challenge. Sometimes we need to stay on task, but sometimes it's even more important to help someone else.

A wise lesson is in learning that the shortest route to victory may be a trap that can cause us to lose more than we gain. Perhaps the woman who stopped to help the fallen runner understood this; if she chose the seemingly clearest path for a short-term win she would lose in a way that her hollow victory could never compensate for. She seemed to understand that sometimes when you win, you lose.

The shortest route to victory may be a trap that can cost us more than we stand to gain.

Sometimes When You Lose, You Win

It can be a great feeling to dominate in competition. Winning decisively so that it is clear just how good we are, whether in tennis, bridge, or in our career, can seem pretty wonderful. Sometimes the old saying captures how we feel, "winning isn't everything, it's the only thing."

There are also times when we feel bad for the competition, especially if it is a child, a friend, or a well-liked relative. At one time or another most of us have experienced the wish, and even taken the actions, to lose on purpose. Consequently, we can end up feeling like a winner because of the joy the victory brings to our opponent, especially if it is a child. After all, would you really want to continue to compete if you knew that your continuous victories would bring frustration and dismay to someone you care about?

Most of us have also been in circumstances where winning just seems too easy. In competition when victories come with little challenge, we can find ourselves unmotivated, complacent, and losing interest. Continuous winning can become so routine that it loses much of its value to everyone involved.

An inspiring example of how the experience of losing can actually restore the value of winning can be found in the story of the 2000 U.S. Women's Olympic Softball Team. As the defending Olympic Gold Medal winners, the U.S. team was expected to win easily. In the words of one of the players, Lisa Fernandez, "I thought we were going to come through and show how dominant U.S. softball was."[23]

Consider the facts. The team had:

- Won the 1996 Olympic gold medal

- Eight players returning from the 1996 team

- Just completed an international tour and won all 60 of their scheduled games

- A winning streak going into the Olympics of an incredible 110 straight victories.

Looking to the 2000 Olympics, one might have easily . . . yawn . . . thought it would be a . . . yawn . . .

cakewalk . . . a kind of "so what" victory. After all, they always win, don't they? Well it didn't turn out that way. After beating Canada 6–0 and Cuba 3–0 in the first two games, they proceeded to lose three consecutive games to Japan, China, and Australia. This formerly dominant team was on the brink of elimination. They needed two consecutive clutch victories to even have a chance at a medal. And they would have to face all three of the teams that had beaten them to have a shot at the gold. Suddenly the "cakewalk" had turned into a heroic battle for survival.

How did they respond? Did they throw in the towel? No, they instead used their losses to stage an even greater victory. First, they banded together and took a symbolic group shower in their uniforms to wash away the "voodoo curse." And then they played as hard as they could, focusing on every single pitch, out, and at bat. They proceeded to win five straight victories to recapture the gold medal. Overnight, the unbeatable, always win, "should I even bother to play" Americans had become the heroic "comeback kids." And the fanfare from the media, fans, and the team itself was far greater than anyone imagined it would be. Most everyone seemed to agree that the victory in 2000 significantly surpassed that of 1996.

After losing, this team was ultimately able to win at a whole new level. Their story serves as a reminder to us all that when things are going poorly . . . when we seem to be losing in a bad way . . . we don't need to be demoralized and give up. Things can turn around if we give it our all and persevere. Our temporary loss may just be a prelude to a much sweeter victory in the end.

So remember, sometimes your losing can be a gift to a child or friend that allows them to experience joy and confidence because of their victory. And sometimes when you lose at first but persevere and try your best to turn things around, your ultimate victory can be all the greater. Sometimes when you lose, you win.

Persevere in the face of a short-term loss … it could be the prelude to an even greater victory in the end.

10

Succeed At Win/Win, Not Win/Lose

There are many ways to win. Some ways involve a heavy emphasis on our own wishes and a use of power, intimidation, and even force to get what we want. This approach can be described as win/lose. Our gain is at the expense of others and in order for us to win, others must lose. The classic win/lose example is in competitive sports. As teams vie to be the victors, they win by handing losses to other teams.

Everyday life is also filled with potential win/lose situations such as disagreements, misunderstandings, or when more than one person wants the same thing—whether it's a last piece of sale clothing or to be chosen from many candidates for promotion into a single open job position. Unfortunately, such win/lose encounters can be demoralizing and damaging to relationships.

A perspective designed to avoid the pitfalls of potential win/lose situations has been described as a win/win approach. An attempt is made to satisfy the wishes of all involved, even if their views appear to be in opposition. For example, the Harvard Negotiation Project prescribes several win/win type strategies that are included in the popular book *Getting to Yes*. Among other things it advocates separating the people involved from the problem, focusing on underlying concerns as opposed to stated positions, and reaching agreement based on objective criteria and fair procedures.[24]

Despite the obvious advantages of win/win— multiple people enjoying the satisfaction of winning, the innovation and creativity that tends to emerge from working toward a better solution that satisfies all involved—this can be a difficult strategy to embrace. If you are the one who may not get your way, the promotion or opportunity, or the spoils of victory you worked so hard for, it is easy to fall prey to a win/lose mentality. In doing so, long-term satisfying success can be put at risk.

The experience of Alpha Fitness Center owner and personal trainer Tom Thompson provides a striking example. For several years Tom was in the commercial real estate business, brokering and managing a large number of properties. From all appearances, Tom was quite successful, even prospering, while most others were struggling badly in the face of a major recession in the industry. Thus, when Tom's largest client explained that his organization was consolidating its management and leasing of their properties, Tom was optimistic. He fully expected that he would not only keep his current portfolio but be given responsibility for several additional properties in reward for his successful operation of their real estate. However, a few minutes into the conversation it was clear that his client was painfully struggling with telling Tom that they were terminating his contract. His portfolio was to be given to another real estate firm.

Justifiably, Tom could have been defensive, angry and hostile toward his client, "after all I've done for you and your organization . . . this is outrageous . . . !!!" Instead Tom interrupted his client, relieving him of his agonizing task, and asked if the relationship between the two of them was still good. The client responded by saying that it absolutely was. Tom then explained that he was really in the relationship business rather than the real estate business and if their relationship was still good then he was satisfied. With that he walked away from a sizable and lucrative portfolio of real estate and began his bottom level entry into the fitness business (which, by the way, was Tom's true passion).

A couple years later, when Tom's former client needed someone to run a fitness center to enhance a new commercial property complex, he proceeded to give—not sell, but give—Tom the fitness business. All of the quality fitness equipment and the facility itself were financed by the company and Tom was simply asked to pay back a percentage of the profits from the business. More recently the client's organization decided to give Tom yet another even nicer "state of the art" fitness center which cost upward of a million dollars to finance.

Imagine if Tom had taken a win/lose attitude about the apparent unfair loss he was handed in the highly competitive real estate industry. Had he blown up at his former client, undoubtedly that would have been the end of the story. Instead he focused on how he and his client could both win in terms of their relationship. And this win/win view in the long run helped Tom to enjoy an even more satisfying kind of career success.

**When in conflict, work
to satisfy the others involved
as well as yourself for a better
and more lasting result.**

Succeed at Being a "Tryer" Even When You're a "Failure"

In the 2000 Summer Olympics in Sydney an unlikely hero emerged. I'm talking about Eric Moussambani, a swimmer from Equatorial Guinea. Eric began the sport just nine months before the games, and he trained in a small hotel swimming pool. In fact, his biggest concern during a television interview seemed to be whether he could finish his race, which would be the longest distance he had ever swum.

When the time came for him to swim in his assigned qualifying heat, the two other swimmers in the heat were disqualified for false starts. So he swam the whole race alone in the pool to the wild cheers of hundreds of appreciative spectators.

What great performance brought out the excitement, enthusiastic support, and even a standing ovation from the international crowd? His time was nearly twice that of the fastest qualifying time of the day. He was even slower than the record for the event that is twice as long as his. There is no question that he failed to win the event and to be quite frank, failed badly. But there was also no question that he was a large success in *trying*, and the fans let him know this in loud supportive cheers. These cheers, he believed, enabled him to hang in there, endure, and finish the longest and most grueling swimming race of his life, the 100-meter freestyle (a mere two lengths of the pool).

Fear of failure is one of the biggest obstacles to living a full and rewarding life. Avoiding mistakes or doing a poor job in performing a new activity can cause us to not even try.

Even the best in the world in a given endeavor made many, many, many mistakes on their way to becoming the best. The finest musicians in the world hit many sour notes in their hours and hours of practice. Babe Ruth did hit more home runs than anyone else in his generation, but his strikeouts far outnumbered his homers.

The Olympic Games are one of the greatest symbols of excellence. The best athletes from around the world gather every four years to compete. Much attention and acclaim are bestowed on those who prove to be the best in competition and walk away with the gold medal in their sport. However, in our admiration of these champions we sometimes lose sight of the real purpose and meaning of the Olympics.

It is sad when we see Olympians who have trained to their limit for four or more years, fall during their race, incur a sidelining injury during their final warm-ups, or simply discover that they may be good but they are not quite good enough to beat the best. At those times it's important to remember that the real victory is in the trying and the participation in the challenge. Many have probably never read the Olympic Creed. It captures well the idea that we can succeed at trying even when we seem to fail.

The Olympic Creed

The most important thing in the Olympic Games is not to win but to take part, just as the most important thing in life is not the triumph but the struggle. The essential thing is not to have conquered but to have fought well.

—Baron Pierre de Coubertin,
the founder of the modern Olympic Games

Help Others Win, Even at Your Own Expense, to Help Yourself

I t's nice to win. The recognition, adulation, and sense of accomplishment can be almost intoxicating. This feeling can cause us to place a huge emphasis on achieving victory for ourselves in order to keep these good feelings coming.

Sometimes, however, it's even better to enjoy the victories of others, especially those we care about. Most everyone knows the joy of watching children who are important to us win in sports, a spelling bee, a music competition, or even a silly game at a county or state fair. And we are often ready to sacrifice our own benefit to help kids in situations like this to win. Certainly most parents know this feeling—we want our kids to be winners. That desire is most often for their benefit and happiness rather than just our own ego satisfaction.

Similarly, when we choose to mentor someone who is less experienced in an area where we possess expertise, we want them to win. We sincerely hope that they will grow in their work and career and ultimately experience significant success. The same goes for valued friends, colleagues, and teammates. It can be very satisfying to help someone else win at work and in life, even when it means we have less time and effort to attend to our own immediate success. Perhaps the real winners in life are persons who have not only succeeded in their own efforts but were able to look beyond themselves and help others win as well.

Consider the case of Steve Jobs and Apple Computer. Known to be a hard-driving, avid competitor, Jobs returned to the helm of Apple in 1997, after more than 10 years away. In business, one way executives keep score to measure their level of victory is through their salary level and amount of accumulated wealth. But Jobs refused any pay or stock. Instead he received a token $1 salary. In an interview Jobs explained, "I didn't return to Apple to make a fortune . . . . I just wanted to see if we could work together to turn this thing around when the company was literally on the verge of bankruptcy. The decision to go without pay has served me well."[25]

Eventually, Apple did turn around and Jobs benefited substantially in a financial way.[26] This result demonstrates an interesting feature about life and a common theme I have heard many motivational speakers and writers echo over the years—if we help others get what they want, we usually get much of value ourselves. Upon his return to Apple, Jobs seemed to focus much more on helping the company and its employees succeed and apparently was less concerned about his own victory on the executive wealth playing field. And helping others win, initially at his own expense, helped him to be a significant long-term winner at Apple, both financially and as a person.

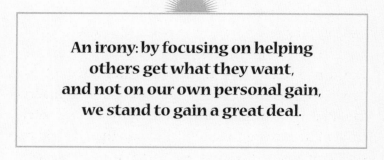

An irony: by focusing on helping others get what they want, and not on our own personal gain, we stand to gain a great deal.

Lose a Disagreement
To Build a Relationship

If you can keep your head when all about you
Are losing theirs and blaming it on you,
If you can trust yourself when all men doubt you,
But make allowance for their doubting too ...
—From "If" by Rudyard Kipling

People are almost always the key to a more rewarding and successful life. Unfortunately (or if you master a wiser view, thank God) people are different and frequently disagree.

When we find ourselves in one of these disagreements, we are presented with the golden seeds of opportunity in what at first glance looks like the weeds of misfortune. The key is to resist the compulsion to always try to win. There is a time to win and a time to lose. At least it may seem that you lose. But, as pointed out in Chapter 9, sometimes you can actually win by losing.

By acknowledging the logic of someone's differing point of view, and allowing their argument to carry the day, you present them with a special gift. We all need to feel "right" some of the time, and each person's perspective usually has value if you really look for it. That means there is a good chance that they are indeed right, even if you happen to be right too.

I have found this to be an invaluable perspective in my writing with co-authors. Most of my books and articles were completed with co-authors—sometimes our perspectives are surprisingly similar and we disagree about very little. More often, we have very different views and sometimes they come into direct conflict.

At first, I struggled with these disagreements, which often led to tension and defensiveness. Over time, though, I have learned that if there is no disagreement, we as co-authors are likely redundant and may not all be needed on the project. I have learned to curb my natural tendency to argue for my point of view and to spend more time trying to listen and understand. Even when I am still convinced I'm more "right" then they, if the issue seems more important to my colleagues and their perspectives seem acceptable (although perhaps to me not optimal) I will go with their viewpoints. Subsequently, the commitment and quality of the work they bring to the project seems to be genuinely enhanced and the author team as a whole is better off.

The idea is not to always "wimp out" and become unassertive. Rather it's to choose your victories and your gracious seeming defeats wisely. Remain assertive for the really important things, but learn how to see the difference between trivial ego victories and championing meaningful causes.

You will build better relationships and earn respect by being respectful. Sometimes losing a disagreement in the short term is a building block to longer term success with people.

When you have a disagreement with others, there is a good chance that they are right, even if you happen to be right too.

When You Feel That You're "Losing It," Declare "Temporary Sanity"

When we feel really out of sorts and are totally "losing it," it is very difficult to keep any semblance of a balanced and healthy perspective. It could be that we are very angry at someone close to us or feel we have been mistreated by a boss or co-worker. Or we are confronted with a major area of anxiety and fear in our lives.

It is natural to get washed away by all the emotion that is released. We may go into a tirade or withdraw and shut ourselves off. We tend to see things from only our limited point of view and how the situation affects us personally: "if he had any respect for others, he would know how unreasonable he is being and agree with me!" This inner loss of control usually leads to outer loss in our current situation.

At times like this, when we are really worked up and upset, in a very real sense we are acting from a state of temporary insanity. This phrase has become a bit of a cliché that many view as simply a way to duck responsibility or to avoid suffering legal recourse from a destructive act. At the same time it raises a valuable alternative possibility.

When we are beginning to feel insanity coming on or have already been sucked into its powerful vortex, we can simply declare a period of "temporary sanity." That is, we can step back from the situation and our immediate reactions and recognize what is happening to us—that we are no longer thinking clearly or constructively. Once we can recognize this, we can declare that we now choose, for the next one, two, five, or more minutes, to see things sanely, even trying to empathize with the other person's point of view.

The following example is based on my observations of many workplace feuds over the years. Sally Fleming had a history of destructive conflict with Fred Herds, a colleague in her work area. They simply didn't see eye to eye and had a knack for pressing each other's emotional buttons. Eventually Sally recognized the repeated pattern and how her own angry and irritated reactions seemed to feed Fred's. She also recognized how their unhealthy conflict interfered with the performance of their work team. Sometimes their arguments dominated problem-solving discussions.

So Sally decided to stop feeding the feud. When she recognized growing tension and her own anger, she declared "temporary sanity" and went silent for a few moments. Sometimes she even counted to ten while reminding herself to "be sane." This silence in turn seemed to calm Fred and he stopped his own pushing. Consequently, most of these disagreements seemed to work themselves out as others contributed additional perspectives that often met both Sally's and Fred's concerns. Over time Sally and Fred became close and respectful colleagues. When the old pattern of conflict would re-emerge, Sally would simply declare "temporary sanity" once again.

This declaration can be a great exercise in effective self-leadership—to recognize our ranting, pouting, or saddened ego and choose to act constructively for a set period of time. Very often this mere act will help us to recognize the futility of our current reactions and help us to transcend them. And this recognition can benefit all we come in contact with. Even if it doesn't, it will likely limit the amount of damage we cause, at least for a short period of time, and help us to better manage our reactions and emotions in the future.

So the next time you feel yourself tumbling out of control toward an emotional fit of temporary insanity, stop, study yourself, and then declare a few moments of temporary sanity!

Stepping back from emotionally charged situations and choosing to be "sane" can limit damage and help build relationships.

The greatest mistake you can make in life is to be continually fearing you will make one.[27]

—*Elbert Hubbard*

Part
Three

Coping with Failure

Sometimes failure is failure, at least in the short run. If we can learn to accept failure as a necessary part of life and then take from it the valuable lessons it offers, we can transcend it. Sometimes it's best to not try to deny or redefine failure but to effectively cope and cooperate with it for future success.

Accept When Failure
Is Really Failure

Author Sydney Finkelstein recently wrote an article in which he outlined several factors that contributed to the dot-com collapse of 2000–2001.[28] Among those was an apparent overly positive embrace of failure as an end in itself. Finkelstein points out that the assumption that failure will necessarily lead to learning is not always true. Many Internet company executives, especially young and inexperienced ones, developed a cavalier attitude toward failure, taking actions that were quite harmful to their firms. From Finkelstein's view, real failure, rather than adaptive long-term-oriented learning, was the dominant result.

Throughout this book I have tried to make it

clear that what we call failure is usually only a temporary setback or a "challenge in progress." Sometimes, however, failure really is failure and we need to accept it for what it is. This requires that we face it honestly and avoid going too far to redefine it. Don't get me wrong, I'm not going to reverse this book's theme 180 degrees and suddenly say that we should look at failure as a dead end and as a trigger for guilt and remorse. Rather, I'm saying we need to recognize that sometimes failure is just that—failure—so we need to face it honestly, take from it what we can, and get on with moving beyond it.

When is failure really failure? The answer to this question largely depends on the person. Perhaps the most obvious answer is when we do not learn anything from a setback that can help us progress toward success in the longer run. But here are some other criteria to consider that cast a different light on the issue. Failure is failure when we:

- Choose an unethical or immoral act

- Act selfishly in a way that harms others

- Perpetrate an intentional destructive deception on others

- Commit to something and don't follow through, not because of an honest mistake or personal lack of current capability, but because we don't make a sincere effort to honor our commitment.

I'm sure most of us can identify with some of these criteria, but the key factor is that we don't make honorable choices. A classic historical example is contained in the story of David in the Old Testament. David is a legendary figure whose feats included defeating the giant Philistine warrior Goliath in battle, becoming King of Israel, and authoring many Psalms.

After becoming king, David had an affair with the married woman Bathsheba and arranged for her husband to be killed in battle so that he could marry her himself. Ultimately, David was able to openly and honestly admit that he had made a dishonorable, indeed an immoral, choice and then to face his personal failure. He could not undo much of the destruction he had caused, but he did go on to make changes in his life to return himself to a more noble path. Historical accounts indicate that David's reign as king did not begin to reach its peak until after he accepted and faced his failure—his affair with Bathsheba and the murder of her husband.

For more recent examples we can look to presidential scandals such as the controversy surrounding Clinton's extramarital behaviors or Nixon's Watergate cover-up. It wasn't until both of these men were able to admit and face their failures that the wounds could be cleaned and healing could begin. There is no question that such actions can leave deep scars, but avoiding long-term infection usually requires that we "come clean" and face our failures.

In the context of business, authors John Slocum, Cass Ragan, and Albert Casey have argued that when CEOs fail, they frequently go through similar stages to those described in literature on death and dying: denial, anger, bargaining, depression, and acceptance. Notably they often get stuck in the denial and anger stages. They refuse to take responsibility for their mistakes and frequently blame and mount attacks on others. As a result they rarely reach the acceptance stage, which could open them to learning and renewed long-term success.[29]

In most situations what might have been called failure can be transformed into a stepping-stone to success. But sometimes it is something else—real failure—and we need to face that we have failed. Until we do, we can find ourselves sinking deeper and deeper into a darkness tied to the past rather than rising toward a brighter future. Our long-term success may well depend on our accepting, in the short run, when failure is really failure.

Honestly facing our "real failures" can help free us from a dark past and prepare us for a bright future.

Choose to Be Happy Over Being Right

Life can be pretty frustrating when it fails to deliver what we think it should. When our new computer software doesn't work quite the way it was supposed to, when the waiter brings our sandwich with mayonnaise when we asked for mustard, or when the new phone service doesn't completely deliver what we thought it promised, we may feel it is time to fight for "what we deserve!" The personal loss or the inconvenience may be relatively minor but "it's the principle of the thing!" Inevitably, though, there is cost in terms of time, effort, and unhealthy stress from waging the battle.

At these times it's a good idea to ask the wise question "do I want to be right or to be happy?" Sometimes being right is worth the fight—if you're

allergic to the mayonnaise you need to send the
sandwich back, even if it temporarily puts a damper
on the lunch atmosphere for your party. Standing up
for what you think is right may provide a significant
opportunity to share perspectives, learn, and come to
a win/win solution that benefits all involved. But
often, if you're honest with yourself, you will be happier and healthier if you simply make the best of the
situation. Sometimes accepting a failure to get what
we feel we rightfully deserve in specific circumstances can help us live more successfully overall.

Imagine the following situation involving two
peers who work together. Katlyn has a significant difference of opinion with Melissa about how department meetings should be handled. Melissa prefers
that a specific agenda be established ahead of time
and one person be designated timekeeper to monitor
progress to assure that each meeting adheres to a pre-
set schedule. Katlyn prefers a more relaxed approach
that relies on a loose agenda but allows for meetings
to drift to different topics as interest and insights
arise from the group and for the time allotted to each
issue to naturally adjust as the meeting unfolds.

Recently, meetings have been conducted based
on the model Melissa supports, but on this particular
day Katlyn decided to raise the issue with her pri-
vately. Melissa's response was immediate and strong,
"If we try your approach, we'll never get anything
done and our meetings will last forever. I'm sorry,
Katlyn, but I just think it's a very bad idea."

Katlyn made a quick assessment of the situation. She realized that Melissa had a great deal of passion about this issue since she had spent a lot of time and effort in researching the literature on effective meetings and designed the current format being used in the department. Katlyn also recognized that Melissa was a good colleague who worked hard and was usually very supportive of others. She also did feel that department meetings were generally effective. Her biggest concern was that the emphasis on meeting structure tended to discourage creativity and innovation. But she also recognized that many impromptu meetings sprang up all the time that resulted in creative and innovative efforts. Rationally she concluded that letting Melissa be "right" this time and retaining the current meeting approach was not really that much of a problem. In fact, it was probably helpful in many ways. After all, they had a pretty demanding workload and efficient meetings helped free up time to keep up with the demands.

Nevertheless, Melissa's direct criticism was quite ego bruising and stirred up hurt and angry feelings in Katlyn. And Katlyn, despite being a generally cooperative person open to different ideas, also felt she had a good sense of how people worked well together and she usually wasn't shy about asserting her opinion. Also, she did feel she was right about her viewpoint in this case.

Ultimately, she decided that confronting Melissa further would only encourage a battle of egos that could cause tension between them for days. She still felt her position was right, but once she got beyond her ego she recognized that Melissa was right too. In the end she decided to drop the issue. In this case trying to convince Melissa that she was "right" just wasn't worth the cost. Nor did she believe the additional learning that might result from further discussion of the issue would compensate for the relationship difficulties it would stir up. Many other issues represented better opportunities to assert herself with greater potential benefits.

These kinds of situations provide us with valuable occasions to accept that the world and the imperfect people in it often don't fit neatly with our preferences but that we can positively deal with this reality. After all, what good is it to prove yourself right and to succeed at getting "what you deserve" if it only makes you unhappy? Make a commitment to yourself to choose being happy often, even when you have to forgo "being right." When you realize how much frustration and stress it eliminates, you will in fact find that it is the *right* thing to do.

> **When you find yourself in a battle of egos, learn to ask: "Do I want to be happy or to be right?"**

17

Use EQ to Cooperate With Failure... to Succeed

Significant attention has been focused on the concept of emotional intelligence (EQ) made popular by Daniel Goleman in his book *Emotional Intelligence*.[30,31] Research in this area suggests that a person's EQ can be as important as IQ (Intelligence Quotient) for determining effectiveness and success. Among other strengths, people with higher EQ tend to be more perceptive of hidden opportunities and interpersonal challenges that need to be addressed. By tapping into our emotional energy and our intuition, emotional intelligence can allow us to move beyond our success capacity based on only rational and intellectual intelligence. Part of the challenge is to see our emotions as sources of useful information for success and even wisdom as opposed to distracting intrusions. Since our emotions are highly interconnected with our thoughts, effectively managing our thought patterns is key.

One way to begin working with this important source of potential success is to take a piece of paper and draw a line down the middle creating two columns. Identify a disturbing situation involving either a past or potential failure that seems to be negatively affecting your thinking and emotions. List

"Emotional Intelligence" refers to the capacity for recognizing our own feelings and those of others, for motivating ourselves, and for managing emotions well in ourselves and in our relationships. It describes abilities distinct from, but complementary to, academic intelligence, the purely cognitive capacities measured by IQ. Many people who are book smart but lack emotional intelligence end up working for people who have lower IQs than they but who excel in emotional intelligence skills.

—*Daniel Goleman,*
from Working with Emotional Intelligence[32]

your dysfunctional thoughts about the situation in one column and list alternate, more constructive thoughts in the other.

For example, after making a presentation at work that seemed to go poorly you might find yourself thinking,

> *I really blew it. I came across as unprepared, inarticulate and incompetent. I am a lousy presenter.*

Then, after carefully examining your reactions to the situation, you could challenge your thinking with more constructive thoughts, such as

> *Actually, given that I only had two days to prepare and that I never had a chance to do a practice run-through of my presentation, I did pretty well. I did convey the ideas I wanted to fairly clearly. I just made a mistake in telling my opening story and I confused two points later in the presentation that caused me to become flustered. It may not have been the best presentation ever made but I can learn from this and in the future I will rehearse my presentations ahead of time.*

Through this kind of internal analysis we can begin to manage our immediate thoughts and feelings. In the process we set ourselves up for the kind of constructive actions that can help us to be more successful in the future.

In Chapter 2 I shared some of Bill Gates's thoughts on the importance of turning failures into successes. Some of his comments on the challenge of managing thinking in the face of difficulties fit well with the topic of emotional intelligence. "It's all in how you approach failures. And believe me, we know a lot about failures at Microsoft. . . . The weight of all of our failures could make me too depressed to come in to work. Instead I am excited about the challenges and by how we can use today's bad news to help solve tomorrow's problems."[33]

This kind of thinking is consistent with the viewpoint advocated by Peter Senge in his classic book *The Fifth Discipline: The Art & Practice of the Learning Organization*. He explains that there is a tendency for organizations to experience decline as members lower their vision in order to eliminate emotional tension caused by falling short of their objectives. According to Senge, in the organizations that thrive, members tend to master a kind of creative tension where instead of experiencing the negative emotions of failure they come to see things differently. "Failure is simply a shortfall, evidence of a gap between vision and reality . . . an opportunity for learning."[34] Consequently, these firms take action to close the gap between the vision and the current performance level and rise, rather than decline, in the face of setbacks.

One could argue that Bill Gates's tremendous

run of success at Microsoft stems largely from his emotional intelligence. Instead of being emotionally paralyzed by setbacks, his perspective reveals a sound way, both intellectually and emotionally, for dealing with potential failures. When we adopt this kind of emotionally intelligent approach, it can help us to adjust and learn as we go so that we too can harness the *Power of Failure*.

Let Mental Storms Blow Through

L et's face it, the quality of our life experience is greatly affected by our moods. Even when we seem to be succeeding in life outwardly (in our work, relationships, health), we can experience a kind of inner failure and find ourselves feeling down. We may just wake up on the wrong side of the bed or dwell on disturbing thoughts about past or possible future failures.

At these times remember that our moods come and go and usually have little significance. True, we can feed them with additional worry, frustration, sadness, or some other emotion and cause them to grow in their intensity until they really do seem like a big deal. On the other hand, if we just let the mood pass we will find that those gloomy thoughts will give way to the more desirable ones that are right behind them.

An effective way to think about this is to view our thoughts and moods as inner storms. When a rainstorm blows in, we can get upset, shake our fist, and yell at it. Or we can just watch it run its course with mild interest and with full awareness that the sun will soon come out again. The same goes for our inner storms. A poetic image of this view follows.

Inner Storm

A distant rumble, a flash of light,
a mental storm portends.
A gust of wind, a hail that bites,
when will it ever end?

I brace myself and tighten my hold
upon a hopeful view.
But those thoughts bring forth a stormy night
of mental servitude.

I arch my back and tense my fists
of thoughtful discipline.
And all the while the storm uproots
the peace that holds me in.

I do respect the outer storms
and let them run their course.
So why allow the inner storms
to cause me such remorse?

It's a fight I cannot win.
How can I stop the night?
But simply let it blow on through
and I regain my inner sight.

—*Charles C. Manz*

If we see moods and negative thoughts as simply symptomatic of inner weather—mere storm fronts that will soon run their course on their own if we don't feed them—then we are better able to keep things in perspective. The challenge is to not attach too much importance to a temporary mood. By allowing these mental storms to blow on through, we allow our dark inner clouds to give way to inner light once again and the inner and outer success it can bring.

Use Failure to Master Yourself

Few things can be more difficult than finding yourself failing in the heat of battle. Use this to your advantage. When you feel yourself faltering, practice staying calm and thinking clearly. Try to react coolly. You can breathe more deeply and slowly, picture a relaxing scene, or use calming internal self-talk. Use whatever techniques are most effective for you. This is a wonderful self-development exercise.

Most skills are not very useful if they fizzle out in the face of real challenge. Who needs special skills when things are going fine? It's when you feel yourself sinking in the quicksand of impending failure that you most need your wits about you to find any possible way out. Panic and flailing about will only cause you to sink faster.

In my career as a writer, consultant, and professor, I frequently speak in front of groups although I am not a naturally extroverted person. In fact, public speaking is a very difficult challenge for me that can create a great deal of stress in my life. My natural tendency is to feel self-conscious and to be anxious about the possibility of making mistakes in front of the audience. Nevertheless, I have grown to appreciate the valuable opportunity I have every time I speak to further develop my self-leadership. And my speaking has improved significantly as a result.

Sometimes I pause and concentrate on taking a deep relaxing breath, especially if I feel the presentation is not going as smoothly as I would like. Deep slow breathing in and out of the lower abdomen is one of the most healthy and natural techniques available for achieving calm and clarity. Other times I concentrate on tensing and then relaxing certain muscles in my body—in my feet, hands, stomach, and even my face. Simple exercises such as these, when I am in the heat of public performance, have helped me to progress toward mastery of my reactions to tense and challenging situations. I still have a way to go, but often the most challenging and stressful moments afford me the best opportunity to refine my skills.

As you learn to manage your emotional and physical reactions well in the short run, you increase your ability to achieve success in the long run. So when potential failure threatens your composure, practice composing yourself. You can grow your self-leadership muscles by using the challenge of potential failure as your exercise equipment for future success.

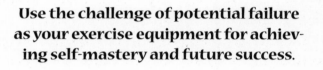

Use the challenge of potential failure as your exercise equipment for achieving self-mastery and future success.

Discover Success at the Point of Maximum Pessimism

We all face times when things seem really bad, even hopeless. At these moments it is easy to become discouraged and to view the situation as strictly a negative obstacle to success and happiness. But many of these situations are actually valuable opportunities for greater success disguised as pending failures. The old expression "It's always darkest before the dawn" points to the opportunities that frequently lie just beneath the dark surface.

Sir John Templeton, one of the greatest financial investors of the twentieth century, recognized this potential. The basis for his tremendous financial success is a philosophy that the best time to invest is at "the point of maximum pessimism." In other words, he has advised acting in ways that seem counterintuitive. Instead of trying to go where the outlook is best, he has searched the world for places where the outlook is most bleak, where others are scared and fleeing from a particular market.

Some of the notable examples of Templeton's against-the-tide investments include Japan in the 1960s when people thought the Japanese market was a mess and it would be crazy to invest there, Ford Motor Company in the late 1970s when the future looked very bleak for the auto giant, and Peru in the mid-1980s when political tension gripped the country and money and the middle class were fleeing. He committed significant sums in each of these cases and just a few years later earned millions on these investments.[35]

Templeton saw significant stock market drops, which sent others into panic selling, as golden opportunities to invest. The best time to buy is when everyone is selling, the price is low, and there is almost nowhere to go but up, was the logic he espoused. This perspective extends to many other difficulties beyond financial investing. When things have hit bottom in some aspect of our lives, we have an opportunity to rebuild, to try something new and fundamentally different, to make an investment when there is little left to lose and a lot to gain.

Throughout history human beings have resisted change that threatens their current comfort zone. That is, until things start to go bad and that comfort zone becomes quite uncomfortable indeed. Personal relationships, for example, can get in a monotonous rut. But when conflict springs up, and things get difficult, the motivation to change is created. And often the closest bonds between people result from facing a crisis together.

Many of the greatest innovative breakthroughs have resulted from formidable problems that arose that needed to be solved: spectacular medical advances from the onslaught of serious illnesses and injuries; revolutionary new construction strategies and materials from the threat of horrific storms and earthquakes; powerful new energy sources and vastly more efficient cars and machinery from serious shortages and environmental dangers; and even effective strategies of diplomacy from crises between groups and nations.

So when things get bad and pessimism abounds, don't panic and back off. Remember, it was gravity itself that ultimately challenged and motivated us to fly. Instead of retreating, move in closer and look very carefully. Search for the treasures that can produce life's greatest success opportunities when difficult circumstances are upon us time and again.

When pessimism abounds, don't retreat … move in and look for the treasures that difficult circumstances create for success.

Both Beauty and Ugliness Are in the Eye of the Beholder

"Beauty is in the eye of the beholder" is an old and familiar saying. In the Introduction, the story of the Ugly Duckling was discussed as a potent metaphor for key elements of the *Power of Failure*. In the story a bird that was shunned and thought ugly because he was so different from the other ducks turned out to be a beautiful swan. The story can inspire us to see that emerging beautiful-swan-like successes are often simply disguised as ugly duckling short-term failures.

In this context we need to add to that old expression: "Both beauty and ugliness are in the eye of the beholder." This is a very important idea. Every time we perceive a problem, worry, concern, or failure—

an ugly duckling of any kind—we need to understand that any negativity is first and foremost in our minds.

Each of us has a different reality in our own head. For example, I frequently have interesting conversations with my college-age son about movies. I tend to enjoy many of the popular "big box office successful" movies that create powerful illusions of reality and draw the audience into the film. My son very much likes films that stretch the limits of the norm, even for his age group. He enjoys independent films of the avant-garde genre that break with the idea of illusion and violate many popular film characteristics. Many of these movies, while rich in symbolism and artistic expression, have very little of the "beautiful" scenery and captivating story line that I value most in a movie but that he sees as unoriginal. And they tend to be only modest financial successes; in fact, many might say they are box office failures.

My son does not like what he describes as formulaic and predictable Hollywood movies. He sees many of the biggest box office successes as artistic failures. What I, and many others, see as a beautiful and very successful epic movie he sees as an ugly duckling indeed.

Each of us encounters these perceptual distinctions throughout our lives. If we are asked to make a speech, some of us will view it as a beautiful opportunity to successfully express our views and share what we know. Others will view it as a personal crisis, an occasion for failure that will publicly expose the embarrassed and unacceptable ugly duckling that we think we are.

These distinctions challenge us to look and look again at every situation we view as ugly for the beauty that is likely there but that we have a hard time seeing. One strategy is to simply ask for the insights of others who tend to think a bit differently than we do—"what possible opportunities do you see in this situation that I am struggling with?" Even more to the point, we can challenge ourselves to rethink the situation, to remember that beauty and ugliness are in the eye of the beholder. This rethinking builds awareness that negative and positive, ugliness and beauty, often exist only in our minds, and while beauty may be currently hidden to us, it exists nevertheless. This awareness can help us to gain the motivation and courage we need to move forward in the face of these seeming ugly duckling short-term failures that find their way into our lives day after day.

The beauty of a difficult situation may be hidden from your view, but that doesn't mean it isn't there ... keep looking.

*"Virtually nothing comes out right the first time. Failures, **repeated** failures, are finger posts on the road to achievement. The only time you don't want to fail is the last time you try something. . . . One fails forward toward success."*[36]

—*Charles F. Kettering*

Part
Four

Collaborating
With Failure

Successful failure can become an important part of living a full and successful life. Every significant new venture, new skill learned, or exciting opportunity pursued will bring with it the likelihood of experiencing short-term failures along the way. These setbacks can become important building blocks of success. Learn to be on the lookout for ways to use *The Power of Failure* everyday to live a more prosperous, productive, and peaceful life.

Fail Small
to Succeed Big

One of my favorite stories is the famous account of how 3M came to develop Post-it notes. Initially, the expenditure of significant human and financial resources to develop a new type of glue resulted in failure. The project managed only to create a rather unsticky inferior form of glue. At this point it would have been easy to declare the effort a complete failure and discontinue the project.

One 3M employee, however, continued to work with the glue and discovered a simple but powerful way to use this failure. When he applied the glue to small strips of paper, he stumbled on a breakthrough. He created useful bookmarks that could be used in his hymnal as he sang in the church choir. They were also handy for recording short notes.

After first marketing the discovery only internally to other 3M employees, their positive response led to a whole new product. This simple idea, addressing a very basic human activity, led to a significant success and it all resulted from what appeared to be a failure. The rest is history. A virtual money tree was created that has netted 3M millions upon millions of dollars and enabled them to provide very practical assistance to countless people around the world.

One way to increase your success in your work and life is to master the principle of failing small to succeed big. This wise approach is based on viewing every failure as the foundation for a larger success. Obviously, when we make a small mistake on some activity or task, we can learn from the experience to accomplish greater success later. If we muff a golf shot from a sand trap, we can study what happened. Learning how we can make better shots from sand traps in the future can help us progress toward being an accomplished golfer.

One important point is that what defines a failure as small is relative. The key is to view failures, even ones that seem relatively large at the time, as smaller stepping-stones toward larger successes. When you face pending or actual failure, study it from all angles and take an attitude that the current situation reflects a relatively small cost that will somehow contribute to a larger success. Then work to apply whatever benefits can be gained from the failure to creating future success. While this strategy will not guarantee that your current setback will lead to a larger success, it should increase the probability of this result significantly.

Once again we find ourselves face to face with the importance of failure for success. To become more and more successful, learn the important art of tapping into failures, no matter their size, for even larger successes. When this view is mastered, most of the failures that you experience will take on a whole new light—they will simply become opportunities to fail small to succeed big.

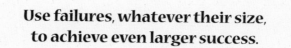

Use failures, whatever their size, to achieve even larger success.

See the Magnificent in the Minimal

When life gives us much less than we wanted or expected, it is easy to get discouraged. We exercise and eat well for weeks and lose far fewer pounds and inches than we had hoped for. We work very hard for many days on a project and only one or two people notice and thank us rather than the multitude we thought would be singing our praises. On such occasions it is easy to lose sight of success and to feel that life has failed us.

But life does not have to give us all we want and expect and rarely does. The key is to learn how to see the possibilities and value in what we do receive and have, even the smallest things. Of all the lines ever written, among my favorite are these by William Blake:

To see a world in a grain of sand
and a heaven in a wild flower,
hold infinity in the palm of your hand
and eternity in an hour.

These lines imply a whole new way to live; a way in which every apparent disappointing failure glows with a bright and beautiful possibility within. For an expanded artistic view of this idea, consider the following poem inspired by Blake's words.

Worlds Within

I walk along a sandy road
and contemplate a thought,
to see a world in a grain of sand,
a broad perspective sought.

"But why not worlds?" I ask myself,
many in each grain.
To see whole universes there
in every single thing.

I look then down beneath my feet
at the endless grains.
And suddenly I find myself
transcending all life's pains.

I see a rainbow in a leaf,
a moonbeam in a stone,
lightning in a withered stick,
and vast heavens in a cone.

I walk then on the sandy road,
shiny gleam upon my eye,
and deep within the gleam does show
that I will never die.

—Charles C. Manz

If we can learn to live with this kind of fresh perspective, everything is transformed. Seeming failures constantly give way to beautiful success possibilities when we are able to see the magnificent in the minimal.

Succeed at Living in the Present Moment

S tress, negativity, depression, and mental and emotional dysfunction in general are often rooted in the past or the future. We regret past choices and failures and anguish over what has happened. We worry about what will happen next, how we might fail this afternoon or tomorrow or next week. But the past is gone forever and tomorrow never comes because when it does arrive, it is today.

The solution to all this mental suffering, which we hear from sources as varied as the writings of ancient wise sages to pop psychologists, is to live in the present moment. The challenge, of course, is to figure out a way to accomplish this when the past seems to always be pulling us into its powerful whirlpool of regrets and the future into its frightening images of the unknown.

A useful way to meet this challenge is to think like an artist. When you take an artistic view of things, when you really try to see your environment and your life circumstances so that you can capture them as a work of art, your focus is naturally tuned into the present. Try taking a walk and composing a poem about what you see. The trees, buildings, birds, clouds, everything will invite your study so that you can describe them in poetic form.

At first this kind of exercise might not seem practical, but it is. Most of us spend much of our mental energy on the past or the future throughout our waking moments. Consequently, we miss much of our lives. We just keep reliving our past failures or anticipating our future ones that rarely ever come. An artistic viewpoint can bring out our creativity and help us to see things we never would have seen. It can root us into an optimistic present that washes away unnecessary stress and worry. But be forewarned that the past and the future will be ever diligent in trying to pull us back out of life and into memories or illusions.

I recently tried this exercise during a walk on a country road. It led me both to the freeing present and face to face with the constant imprisoning beckoning of the past and future. Here is the poem that resulted.

To Remember Myself

On the road traveled
I walked along blankly.
Up into the smoky fog I went,
the smoldering earth engulfed me.
Then upon a rippling brook I arrived.
Crystal blood under the smoky fog jolted me
and I began to awaken like a new dawning day.
It had been a long time since I had been really awake.
And then the mountain laurel, snow white, added a crescendo.
I looked higher and rich green leafy tree branches groped for the sky.
I began to jog lightly and the world seemed to open and take me into its womb.
The mountain laurel turned pink as the stream's blood flowed up and fed its crowns.
There were more and more blossoms now and wide awake I saw something that surprised me so I stopped.
In the midst of the smoking earth, crystal glass water, and the blood ripe flowers I saw myself and I was glad.
But my joy was overtaken by a flowing fear that had followed me, as it always did, and engulfed me again.
Then in a trance once more I regained my senses and turned and started back down the road.
Small wild flowers reached out to remind me but I could not remember how to be alive.
I thought of all the burdens of the day ahead and I faded away.
"Damn fog! What was I thinking about?"
I glanced at my watch and now stiffly
hurried down the hill.

—*Charles C. Manz*

Mental failures almost always live in the past or the future. If you want to find mental successes look to the present. Succeed at living in the present moment. It is in the present that even mistakes and temporary failures can soar high above worry, fear, and regret and offer the opportunities for new life.

Continually Invest for Success ... Even in the Face of Failure

Taking risks and investing yourself in challenging circumstances can be very trying. When you put yourself and what you have garnered in life on the line, it can be unsettling indeed. This might involve your professional standing or even your integrity. When major challenges arise, and there is diversity of opinion on what to do, sometimes you have to stake your reputation and take a stand, despite current trying circumstances.

An auto industry executive with personal convictions about the environment, for example, might put herself on the line to champion a promising but financially risky electrically powered car. And she may do so at the very time that business is down and the majority seem to be in favor of higher emissions designs that have succeeded in the past. She is very conscious of the current difficult circumstances for taking this kind of position. Nevertheless, she feels strongly that investments for a cleaner environment need to be made consistently over time and will pay off for everyone in terms of a healthy planet in the future.

Financial investing provides a straightforward metaphor for these ideas. Investing in the stock market can be as unsettling as the most gut-wrenching roller coaster. At the time of this writing one of the best known companies in America saw its stock price plummet almost 50 percent in one day. And this took place after its shares had climbed by several hundred percent over the previous few months.

When you have a substantial amount invested, significant market dips can make a day, a week, even months, or a year, seem pretty gloomy. You might watch your retirement savings fall well below their previous value and feel like you are experiencing a financial failure of great magnitude.

So where is the success opportunity in a situation like this? It's in the power of consistently investing over time, or what is usually referred to as "dollar cost averaging." If, for example, you always have a portion of your paycheck go into well-managed, balanced mutual funds in your retirement plan, stock market dips are like those exciting department store sales we look for in the newspaper.

Consider a specific example. Susan Wells began investing $100 per month into a high-quality balanced fund 20 months ago for a total investment of $2000. During that time, due to a general stock market decline, the price of the fund's shares has dropped from an average price paid by Susan of $20 down to $15. Consequently the value of Susan's $2000 investment today is only $1500. As a new investor, in the face of this 25 percent loss in value, it would be easy for Susan to become discouraged, declare her investment program a failure, and discontinue her $100 per month purchase of shares.

The reality, however, is that this solid fund's shares are probably a better value today than they were in previous months. The same dollars that would have bought only 5 shares before now buy nearly 7 shares of the same quality companies that are held in the fund. And one thing history has repeatedly shown is that the market eventually goes back up to where it was and then some.

Similarly, when other aspects of our lives experience a temporary downturn, that can be the ideal time to invest more. When our status at work declines and we find we are being called on less and less to contribute our expertise, that can be an ideal time to invest in our value. Learning a new computer skill or signing on for training in people skills may be the last thing on our minds when our work life seems to be on the decline. But choosing to invest in our potential value rather than becoming apathetic or backing away from the job can be a timely anecdote. Again, consistently investing—whether it be for greater knowledge, better relationships, or financial return—when things are up or down, can yield many valuable payoffs in life.

So when life seems to be on the decline or the market is looking ugly, just keep on investing. These seemingly improbable investments will likely yield valuable returns sooner than you might have expected.

Continually investing in yourself, whether things are up or down, can yield many valuable payoffs in life.

Sometimes Choose to Get in Over Your Head to Get Ahead

An old strategy for teaching others how to swim was simply to throw them in deep water, over their heads, with little or no instruction. In the process of struggling to keep their heads above water, it was expected that they would manage to figure out how to swim on their own. While this "sink or swim" approach is not widely embraced today, some wisdom can be gleaned from it. Just as muscles will not get stronger and grow unless exerted beyond their relaxed comfort level, we will not grow as people unless we are challenged. And sometimes this challenge can best be created by "getting in over our heads."

An inspiring example is provided by the life

story of Dr. Kenneth Cooper, M.D. One of his colleagues recently described him at heart as just a regular guy (actually his more colorful words were "a good ole boy from Oklahoma"). Dr. Cooper himself has indicated that he really expected to simply have a relatively small medical practice and perhaps a rather unremarkable life. Instead here are just a few of the things he has done.[37] He:

- Literally wrote the book on aerobics, popularizing this, at the time, revolutionary concept.

- Founded the Cooper Aerobics Center—a state-of-the-art campus that houses the Cooper (research) Institute, Cooper Fitness Center, Cooper (medical) Clinic, and the Cooper Wellness Program.

- Founded Cooper Ventures, Inc. and Cooper Concepts, Inc.

- Developed Cooper Complete Multivitamins and Cooper Complete Joint Maintenance Formula.

- Is the personal physician of many CEOs and celebrities, including dozens of professional athletes and President George W. Bush.

- Has written nearly 20 books with a combined total sales of over 30 million copies.

And the list goes on and on.

But the road to these many successes has been very difficult. When examining Dr. Cooper's life history one is left wondering whether, at many critical points of his career, he felt that he might not be up to the task. Given his groundbreaking pioneer spirit, it appears that he got in "over his head" on many occasions and experienced what, from the outside, look like many setbacks and significant, although temporary, failures.

For example, given his advocacy of preventive medicine and healthy diet and exercise beginning in the 1960s, he was frequently criticized by the more "diagnose and prescribe medicine or surgery" medical community. In the late 60s, when his best-selling book *Aerobics* was published, many physicians had been counseling people, especially if they were 40 or older, to avoid significant physical exercise. One expert even proclaimed that "the streets are going to be full of dead joggers if people continue to follow Cooper."[38] And when Cooper advocated an exercise program as part of the rehabilitation process for persons who have suffered a heart attack, he was viewed by many as being essentially crazy—as an exercise fanatic. Now this practice is part of standard medical protocol.[39]

Indeed, there were times when Dr. Cooper's seeming failures challenged him to his limits. Despite his best-selling book *Aerobics*, his small practice in Dallas initially struggled—patients were few and far between. His original modest office was in a Dallas strip mall and had only two rooms. And when the medical board in Dallas learned that he was using a treadmill to conduct stress tests, the members thought he was endangering lives. He was even brought before the board with the intent of censoring him. Feeling very discouraged, and perhaps feeling that he was in way over his head, he seriously considered discontinuing his medical practice. As he discussed this possibility with his wife, Millie, she helped him remember why he was doing what he was doing. He believed with all his heart that his medical practices represented the future of medicine.[40]

Despite his setbacks, Dr. Cooper has relentlessly persisted as a one-man army who continually takes on battles that seemingly cannot be won. And he has gotten the last laugh. Most of his originally scoffed-at recommendations have become accepted good health practices that have now been endorsed by doctors worldwide. His strong commitment to medical research guided and redefined his medical stance all the way. He bombarded members of the established medical community with truckloads of data that gradually began to win them over. "I've worn down the critics . . . there are still a few . . . but compared to 30 years ago it's minuscule. We have overwhelmed them with data,"[41] explains Dr. Cooper.

Perhaps Dr. Cooper's constant commitment to advancing unpopular "ahead of their time" ideas and health strategies in the face of huge opposition is an ideal metaphor for the notion of "getting in over your head to get ahead." Confronting what at times seem like overwhelming challenges, wrestling with them and personally growing (and helping others to grow) as a result, may be a key secret to great success.

One might ask where the story goes from here. Given all the challenges and accomplishments that this "regular guy" from Oklahoma has already taken on, what can he do as an encore? What challenge is left for him to face, to continue his bold tendency to get in over his head to get ahead? The answer, of course, is for this supposed health and exercise fanatic to become the Surgeon General of the United States. And as of this writing he has been nominated for that very office.

Sometimes the capacity for the greatest successes comes from wrestling with large, even overwhelming, challenges.

When You Feel Lost and Demoralized by Your Life Path … Blaze a New One

Sometimes it can feel as if our lives are headed down a dead-end road to failure. Most of us feel as if we are on the wrong life path at least some of the time. Many of the ideas in this book are about rethinking these situations and transforming them, if only in our mind. Often we miss the beauty and opportunity that are barely hidden by the difficulties we face and we simply need to learn to look at things from a new more optimistic slant.

But sometimes we may in fact be living a life that we were not meant to live. Perhaps we want to please others, so we do what we think they want. Or we have been brought up, socialized, and conditioned to approach life in a certain way and make choices that do not really fit us well at all. Usually a deep sense of loss and failure results. When we discover that we are clearly on the wrong path, we need to create one better suited to who we really are. To find meaningful success in our lives we may need to blaze a new road that is better suited to our true nature. Ponder the following poem and how it might relate to your life.

My Road
Along a well worn road today
I walked without a thought,
until I faced the blazing sun
with fiery light so hot.

My face rained tears of silent dread
of carrying my soul along,
this same old tired dusty road
that I had tread so long.

I stopped bewildered in my tracks
and looked past my graveled guide,
through a lush and flowered living wood
that had been always at my side.

I heard a song somewhere within,
a sad spirit serenade.
The words like soured wine did mourn
the price my soul had paid.

"Why this road?" it asked of me,
the question all too clear.

A thought that I had pondered not
as I marched from year to year.

"Don't you see?" it seemed to ask,
"this roadway's much too worn."
"It's not the path on which to walk,
the one for which you're born."

I spied again the thick lush wood.
It to me did call.
But how could my life be out there,
where there is no path at all?

"There is no path," I heard it say,
"because you've not yet gone,
to blaze a pathway meant to be,
the one for which you belong."

I looked again beneath my feet
at the road I gave such trust
and realized it was not my life
painted by footprints in the dust.

I took a breath and then a step,
into the wood I strode,
a bit unsure but alive within,
as I began to make my road.

—*Charles C. Manz*

We need to make the best of the lives that we
have and always be on the lookout for how we can
live them well. A pathway littered with failure can

provide necessary learning and growth for eventual success. Sometimes, though, to discover truly meaningful success we need to look outside our current life path and consider the possibilities of other roads that we may be meant to travel.

So, when you feel lost in continuous demoralizing failure on your life path, consider blazing a new one that leads ever forward, that is built on a solid foundation of learning and benefiting from every setback and shortfall, and that is forged with the courage and strength that comes from a new life commitment to harness *The Power of Failure*.

Getting Started: The Power of Failure Motto

This book has addressed a variety of life and work challenges. More importantly it has offered practical ways for turning setbacks into success. "The New View of Failure" offered in the Introduction included eight key themes that undergird the *Power of Failure* strategies included throughout this book:

1. Redefine Failure.

2. Redefine Success.

3. Learn from Failure.

4. View Failures as Stepping-Stones for Success.

5. Find the Opportunities of Failure.

6. Use Negative Feedback to Your Advantage.

7. Look Beyond Yourself.

8. Persist.

The *Power of Failure* strategies offer prescriptions for a more productive, prosperous, and peaceful life. Hopefully you will select the ones that are most relevant to your own circumstances and begin to apply them regularly in your life. Of course, the realities of everyday life, and especially the setbacks and failures that it throws in our path, can offer severe challenges for successful living. This statement is especially true when we lose sight of the important role that failure plays for living in a way that benefits from all life has to offer.

To begin meeting these challenges more effectively from this day forward, the first step is to make an all important mental shift. The key is to develop a *Power of Failure* perspective on life. Hopefully what you have read in this book has helped you along that path. To further help with this process the brief statement on the following page can be copied and carried with you in your wallet or purse. Even better, commit it to memory. It's titled *The Power of Failure Motto*. Let it sink deeply into your thinking. Allow it to produce lasting profound life change. Never again find yourself helpless in the face of short-term failures. Instead, continually move forward in positive and rewarding ways as you learn to use the *Power of Failure*.

The Power of Failure Motto

Failure is a natural part of everyday life. Failure, at its best, is a stepping-stone to success, a challenge in progress, and the lifeblood of a successful life. Failure offers us the gifts of learning, the means to become stronger and grow as persons, the possibility for change and innovation, and the chance to see whole new opportunities. Failure can provide us with the foundation for long-term success if we learn to redefine it, to use it to win through losing, and to cope and collaborate with it. Ultimately, both failure and success are in the eye of the beholder. We can live successfully by looking beyond ourselves and seeing all the opportunities that the world has to offer those who have the courage to take on new worthwhile challenges and steadily fail toward success. We can truly live successful lives when we dare to harness **The Power of Failure**.

Notes

[1] This quote is taken from *The Book of Positive Quotations* compiled and arranged by John Cook, (New York: Gramercy Books, 1999), p. 510.

[2] Ibid., p. 517.

[3] See the article "Learning From Failure" by Carole Hyatt, *Leader to Leader*, Summer 2001, p. 13.

[4] This chapter was inspired, in part, by material contained in *The New SuperLeadership: Leading Others to Lead Themselves*, by Charles C. Manz and Henry P. Sims, Jr., (San Francisco: Berrett-Koehler, 2001).

[5] See *Bill Gates @ the Speed of Thought*, by Bill Gates with Collins Hemingway, (New York: Warner Books, 1999), p. 185.

[6] See *The Active Life* by Parker Palmer (San Francisco: Jossey-Bass, 1990), p. 23.

[7] This example is included on the audio program *Unlimited Energy* by Peter McLaughlin (Niles, IL: Nightengale-Conant Corporation, 1998).

[8] See the article "Steve Ballmer's Big Moves" by George Anders, *Fast Company*, March 2001, pp. 142–148.

[9] Ibid., p 144.

[10] Ibid., p 144.

[11] *Catch-22* by Joseph Heller (New York: Simon & Schuster, 1955).

[12] This chapter is based on material contained in *The New SuperLeadership: Leading Others to Lead Themselves*, by Charles C. Manz and Henry P. Sims, Jr.,(San Francisco: Berrett-Koehler, 2001).

[13] This example is included in the classic book on the learning organization *The Fifth Discipline* by Peter Senge (New York: Doubleday, 1990), p. 154.

[14] See, for example, Albert Ellis, *A New Guide to Rational Living* (Englewood Cliffs, NJ: Prentice Hall, 1975).

[15] See the article by Daniel Goleman, "Research Affirms Power of Positive Thinking," *New York Times*, February 3, 1987, p. 15N.

[16] Ibid.

[17] This quote was found in *The Book of Positive Quotations* compiled and arranged by John Cook, (New York: Gramercy, 1999) p. 511.

[18] This description of the NASA selection process for astronauts is based on a personal account received from a private communication with Jack Foster, author of *Ideaship* and *How to Get Ideas*.

[19] This quote is taken from *The Book of Positive Quotations* compiled and arranged by John Cook, Gramercy Books, 1999, p. 511.

[20] This chapter is inspired by material from *The Wisdom of Solomon at Work*, by Charles C. Manz, Karen P. Manz, Robert D. Marx, and Christopher P. Neck (San Francisco: Berrett-Koehler, 2001).

[21] Jon Bowen, "True Confessions," *Runner's World*, March 1999, p. 128.

[22] *What Dreams May Come*, Interscope Communications, 1998.

[23] This quote was found in an online article on the Internet under the headline "96 Was Incredible, But This One's Better," written by Dave Krieger , Scripps Howard News Service, *The Commercial Appeal*, September 27, 2000, Sports, p. D4, Dateline Sydney.

[24] See *Getting to Yes: Negotiating Agreement Without Giving In*, 2nd edition, by Roger Fisher and William Ury, with Bruce Patton, editor (New York: Penguin Books, 1991).

[25] See "Apple's One-Dollar-a-Year Man," *Fortune*, January 24, 2000, p. 76.

[26] In fact, Jobs' financial benefits were so great once the company did turn around that he was featured in a controversial article about high CEO compensation titled "The Great CEO Pay Heist" by Geoffrey Colvin, *Fortune*, June 25, 2001 (www.Fortune.com).

[27] This quote is taken from *The Book of Positive Quotations* compiled and arranged by John Cook, Gramercy Books, 1999, p. 511.

[28] For more information see "The Myth of Managerial Superiority in Internet Startups: An Autopsy" by Sydney Finkelstein, *Organizational Dynamics*, in press.

[29] See "On Death and Dying: The Corporate Leadership Capacity of CEOs" by John W. Slocum, Cass Ragan, and Albert Casey, *Organizational Dynamics*, in press.

[30] This chapter is inspired by material contained in *The New SuperLeadership: Leading Others to Lead Themselves*, by Charles C. Manz and Henry P. Sims, Jr., (San Francisco: Berrett-Koehler, 2001).

[31] Daniel Goleman, *Emotional Intelligence*, (New York: Bantam, 1995).

[32] Daniel Goleman, *Working with Emotional Intelligence* (New York: Bantam, 1998).

[33] Bill Gates, with Collins Hemingway, *Bill Gates @ the Speed of Thought*, (New York: Warner Books, 1999), p. 185.

[34] See *The Fifth Discipline: The Art & Practice of the Learning Organization* by Peter M. Senge (New York: Doubleday, 1990).

[35] Lawrence Minard, "The Principle of Maximum Pessimism," *Forbes*, January 16, 1995, pp. 67–74.

[36] This quote is taken from *The Book of Positive Quotations* compiled and arranged by John Cook, Gramercy Books, 1999, p. 511.

[37] The listing of Dr. Cooper's accomplishments is largely based on the article "Bush's Exercise Guru" by Andrew Ferguson, *The Weekly Standard*, May 7, 2001, pp. 12–13.

[38] See the article: "The Father of the Fitness Craze: Dr. Kenneth Cooper" by Laura Muha, *Biography Magazine*, June 2000, p. 92.

[39] This information is based on a personal conversation with Tom Thompson, a colleague of Dr. Cooper's who has served as a fitness trainer at the Cooper Fitness Center.

[40] Muha, "The Father of the Fitness Craze: Dr. Kenneth Cooper" by Laura Muha, *Biography Magazine*, June 2000, p. 94.

[41] Ibid., p. 93.

Index

About the Author

Charles C. Manz, Ph.D., is an advanced practitioner of the art of successful failure. He credits the *Power of Failure* with most of the success he has enjoyed in life. He views himself as a successful person but is quick to point out that he has experienced far more (successful) "failures" than successes in his life and work.

Specifically, he is a speaker, consultant, and bestselling business author. He is currently the Charles and Janet Nirenberg Professor of Business Leadership in the Isenberg School of Management at the University of Massachusetts. Dr. Manz's work has been featured on radio and television and in *The Wall Street Journal, Fortune, U.S. News & World Report,*

Success, and several other national publications. He received the prestigious Marvin Bower Fellowship at the Harvard Business School, which is "awarded for outstanding achievement in research and productivity, influence, and leadership in business scholarship."

He is the author or co-author of more than 100 articles and 12 books including the best-sellers *Business Without Bosses: How Self-Managing Teams Are Building High-Performing Companies*, the Stybel-Peabody prize winning *SuperLeadership: Leading Others to Lead Themselves*, *The Leadership Wisdom of Jesus: Practical Lessons for Today*, and *The New SuperLeadership*. His other books include *The Wisdom of Solomon at Work: Ancient Virtues for Living and Leading Today*, *Mastering Self-Leadership: Empowering Yourself for Personal Excellence*, *Company of Heroes: Unleashing the Power of Self-Leadership*, *For Team Members Only: Making Your Workplace Team Productive and Hassle-Free*, and *Teamwork and Group Dynamics*. His books have been translated into many languages, and featured in book clubs and on audiotape.

Dr. Manz has served as a consultant for many organizations, including 3M, Ford, Motorola, Xerox, the Mayo Clinic, Procter & Gamble, General Motors, American Express, Arthur Andersen, Allied Signal, Unisys, Josten's Learning, Banc One, the American Hospital Association, the American College of Physician Executives, the U.S. and Canadian governments, and many others.